GET IN THE

BOAT

A Step-By-Step
Guide to
Creative,
Everyday,
Reproducible
Discipleship

MATT ULRICH

CONTENTS

CHAPTER 1

VISION: The Why

What if I told you that *with absolute certainty* I could tell you what God's will is for your life. Would you want to hear it?

Give me just a minute and I will. Seriously! But before I do, I want you to think about this concept for a second:

God's will.

What a loaded pair of words. There is so much power and weight in this small phrase. It changes lives and realigns the aimless. It births and ignites purpose in the directionless. Once a Christian truly comprehends God's will for his/her life, everything changes. Vision is catalyzed, passion and purpose ignite like a match on the side of a matchbox, and everything comes into focus. Questioning and wondering are replaced by clarity and certainty. There is a renewed sense of purpose and the all-pervasive thought, "This is what I was made for!" starts to take hold and builds an immovable certainty and faith within a believer's heart and mind.

The men and women who took hold of that truth and built their lives around what the Lord spoke to them became the greats who, over the centuries, have changed the world. They left a lasting legacy that we still talk about today. Why? *Because they knew God's will for their life.*

The sad truth is, however, that the majority of Christians today have absolutely no idea what God's will is for their lives. They may have the passion and desire, but they are missing the direction and the clear call of what the next steps are.

What about you?

Do you have a desire to change the world, but you don't know where to start? Have you ever told God that you would go wherever and do whatever He wanted, but He never gave you a clear call of what that would look like, so you haven't really moved on that desire at all? Without that clarity, most Christians succumb to the conclusion that God's will is elusive and they just don't have the spiritual maturity to figure it out, so they give up trying and simply settle.

But let's make one thing very clear: God's will is not this mystic whisper that only the select few hear after years of pursuing it. God did not set out to make this difficult. He did not make His will an ethereal truth that He would only disclose to the spiritually elite. In fact, I would go so far as to say that God's will is actually painfully obvious and laid out quite clearly in Scripture. It is a universal call, and precisely because of its universality and familiarity, most Christians dismiss it in search for a more personalized and customized way of God speaking to them, thereby missing God's will for them completely!

You see, the only way we understand and know God's unknown will for our lives is when we are obedient to His known will, which He laid out for us in these two key passages in the book of Matthew:

"Teacher, which is the greatest commandment in the Law?"

Jesus replied: "'Love the Lord your God with all your heart and with all your soul and with all your mind.' This is the first and greatest commandment. And the second is like it: 'Love your neighbor as yourself. All the Law and the Prophets hang on these two commandments." - *Matthew 22:36-40*

Then Jesus came to them and said, "All authority in heaven and on earth has been given to me. Therefore go and make disciples of all nations, baptizing them in the name of the Father and of the Son and of the Holy Spirit, and teaching them to obey everything I have commanded you. And surely I am with you always, to the very end of the age." - *Matthew 28:18-20*

So there you have it: God's will for your life wrapped up into 7 verses. Now I know these popular verses have been preached on, studied, and memorized for over two thousand years, so they have become extremely familiar to us, but don't let that take away from the unbridled potential or radical effect they can have on our souls! You will be missing the essence of God's will for your life if you do! So before you dismiss yet another look at these two passages, let's break this down from a distinctive angle and a different light than what you are used to:

The Great Commandment

Love God, love people.

These are two of the most primitive desires and wirings of the human soul. We all want to truly love and to truly be loved. Whether you are the wildest of extroverts or the deepest of introverts, there is an innate desire in all of us to have community, camaraderie, and deep connections with both God and one another. This is manifested in different ways for different people. For some, this desire is revealed through a longing for the deep intimacy that is found in a marriage. For others, this is demonstrated through the desire for a very close relationship with a best friend. For others, it is the instant bond and community that one finds with those of common interests, such as when you join a sports team or are on a mission with others.

We want relationships that allow us to take off our masks and be ourselves, without judgment.

No matter how it expresses itself, it is true for all of us: we are destined for love. We are made in the image of a triune God who is in community with Himself (Father, Son and Holy Spirit), and therefore we too share this desire and longing for that same type of intimate relationship with God and with others. We read stories in the Bible about David and Jonathan and the depth of love they had for one another and we long for that type of deep, covenant friendship rooted in the Lord (1st Samuel 18:1). We read about Joab and Abishai who led two factions of the Israelite army together and fought back-to-back against the Ammonites and the Arameans (2nd Samuel 10:8-12) where they both showed a fierce love and commitment to one another in battle, even to the point of death.

These types of bonds, forged in war and mission, resonate deep within us and point to the longing for relationships that bring about purpose and meaning. Iron truly does sharpen iron, and not in just some cheap religious way. We are looking for someone who is able to speak truth in love to us, to love us when we do not love ourselves, and pull out the best of us in not only our abilities but in our lives. We want to have companions that see things that we don't and are able to celebrate in our victories and share in our grief. We desire to live alongside someone who is able to help us be a better person simply because we are living life together! We want to live and be rooted in love amongst those who are living lives that matter and we want to do the same.

The Great Commission

We all love movies.

Movies allow us to escape reality for a short time and live vicariously through someone else's story. They allow us to dream and imagine what it would be like to lead a revolution (*Braveheart*), or to save the world (*Mission Impossible*), or get the girl (every chick flick out there)! We, in turn, daydream about epic romances or adventures and fantasize about what it would be like to be someone else.

So why is this so appealing? Well, for a lot of us, that is our only real outlet for this type of love and action because there is no *real* adventure happening in our lives, so we settle for vicarious living through fictional characters we see in movies and on TV. Due to the lack of adventure in our own lives, *we settle for someone else's story.*

But this does not truly satisfy our yearning for adventure because we don't really want to live out someone else's greatness! We long for adventure because this is built into our DNA. We were made for risky undertakings and great exploits, but most of us have settled for a very dull and mundane existence. We have replaced the Kingdom dream with the American dream.

Since when did our dreams involve sitting around and being comfortable? No one said when he or she was little, "When I grow up I want to be comfortable and financially secure." No! They wanted to go to the moon or wanted to be the president or something else *that mattered.* This desire was built inside of us when we were young and gets beaten out of us as we get older. We end up settling for a dream that is far inferior to the one God has put inside of us and wired us to want to fulfill.

What was meant to be a life-changing call that drives us has now been watered down to the security of a nice home with a white picket fence. The desire to bring about change has been replaced with a desire for financial security so that you can what - be comfortable and bored in your final years of life?!

Even if it has been years since you felt it, there is a spark inside of you that wants to change the world. There's a part of you that wants to leave a lasting legacy - to be a part of something greater than yourself; something that will bring about systemic and lasting change. It's undeniably in all of us. The question is, how much have we tempered or dismissed that primal call for revolutionary change? Friends, the God of the Bible and the call that He has given us is no fantasy; it is the most compelling reality that you will ever come across and have the opportunity to experience!!

And this is where discipleship comes into play. It is the fulfillment of the God-given desire to do something great with your life; to leave a legacy and a lasting inheritance for generations to come. It doesn't matter if you're a mom of three, a college student, a retiree, or a blue-collar or white-collar worker... this is *your* call!!

I'll just come out and say it: *It is God's will for your life.*

And if you know Jesus, you know that nothing else is going to satisfy you the way discipleship and bringing about His

Kingdom here on earth will. Why do you think He taught His disciples to pray, "On earth as it is in heaven"? This is not just a cute phrase Jesus wanted to coin. It is the only reality that will bring about meaning in a desperately meaningless world full of false hope and empty promises. No amount of money, no amount of security, no amount of success in the world is ever going to come close to bringing the fulfillment and satisfaction that seeing people come to know Jesus and discipling them will bring.

It is in our blood. It is in our DNA. We are called to be a tribe of renegades, not a religion of conformists! We are called to be insurrectionists who upheave the status quo, not just people who merely give mental ascent to the doctrines of Christianity and attend church semi-regularly!!

Listen, I'm not saying that you're not having a good life now. I really do pray that you're having a good life. But I pray even harder that you have a great and adventurous life. I pray that you'll leave a great legacy. I pray that you will not let good get in the way of great and stop the God-given call and commission that He has given you!

Think about a time that you led someone to the Lord, or a time when you've ever discipled someone and seen them have that "Ah-ha!" moment when they really do understand who Jesus is, what grace is, and what God has done for them. If you have ever had a moment like this, then you understand what I'm talking about when I say there's nothing like that in the world. There is no better feeling than to watch a man or woman become the man or woman that God has called them to be and to have the God-given privilege of taking part in his/her faith journey. And if that is new to you, this book is going to help you tap into these aforementioned realities which are truly like nothing else.

Discipleship is the answer to a boring, lifeless existence.

It is God's will for your life.

Now the beauty and divine creativity of this call is that discipleship has no real formula. Discipleship is not a science; it is an art. No two followers of Jesus and their calls are the same. How you fulfill God's will and call on your life is going to be different from anyone else's.

Where we get into trouble is when we simply try to stuff God and His Kingdom into a formulaic box and reproduce what someone else is doing. We aren't called to simply replicate. We are called to create. Discipleship is not a simple formula; it is a life-long call and commitment to fulfill God's will in your unique life journey as you move toward Christlikeness and bring others along to do the same.

Discipleship: The Good and the Bad. ━━━━━━━━

Have you ever been hungry and already made plans to go out to eat with a friend, but neither of you can make a decision on where to go? Finally, you throw out what you feel like is a pretty good option, but your friend says that they don't want to go there. So you throw out another option… that gets shot down, too. So you finally ask, "Well, where do you want to go?" and his/her reply is, "I don't know, but I don't want to go to those places!"

There are some times when the only way to know what you want or what something is, is to know what it is not. The same is true with discipleship. So let's look at some common and gross misconceptions about discipleship.

When you think of discipleship, what comes to mind? If you are like most Christians, when the word "discipleship" gets dropped, you probably think of some of the most famous New Testament discipleship archetypes, such as Jesus and the apostles, or Paul and Timothy.

This is both good and bad.

The good thing is you are thinking about and learning from the best. I mean come on… it's Jesus! You can't get more perfect than that! And Paul was arguably the most effective church planter and disciple-maker of all time, outside of Jesus. Between the two of them, they were and are the standard bearers of discipleship and what it should look like. There is quite a depth and breadth of knowledge, both theological and practical, that we could spend a lifetime gleaning from both of them and their discipleship practices!

Now for the bad part.

In both of these most famous discipleship cases starring Jesus and Paul, the disciple-maker is light years ahead of their disciples in regard to spiritual maturity and experience. This unfortunately sets an unconscious precedent in most of our minds that if we want to do any sort of effective, fruit-bearing discipleship, we have to be at some top-tier level of holiness and leadership that seems unattainable. Most Christians tap out at this point, claiming they are not ready to disciple anyone. Do any of these hesitations sound familiar?

- "I don't feel equipped to make disciples!"

- "I have so much work to do in my own life. How can I disciple someone else?"

- "I have never been discipled, so how can I disciple anyone if I don't know what it looks like?"

Now again, I want to repeat: no discipleship process or journey is going to look the same. The problem is that the majority of Christians try to quantify and formulate discipleship and jam it into a neat and tidy box that it was never meant to be in. And when it doesn't fit, we figure it isn't going to work for us and we disqualify ourselves before we even begin! And herein lies the discipleship dilemma that has stifled disciple-makers for centuries: the misnomer that you have to be as holy and put together as Jesus before you start making disciples.

That is like saying you have to get in shape before you commit to start running on a regular basis. It doesn't make any sense!! The only way to get in shape is to start running. The only way it happens *is when you do it*.

So with that in mind, let's get started.

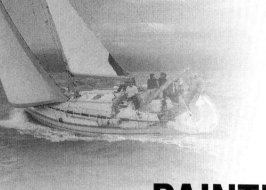

CHAPTER 2

PAINTING THE PICTURE: The What

I love having creative friends. I am personally more of a logical thinker, so it's always good for me to make sure I am rubbing shoulders with creative thinkers every now and then. I was recently talking to one such friend, Czar, about discipleship. Now Czar is the kind of guy who always uses images to describe the point he is trying to convey. So as we talked about discipleship and how that plays out in our lives, he said, "Imagine our pursuit of Christ as being a journey across the sea. We are all swimming or sailing from one side of the sea to the other, with Christ and Christlikeness being the final destination on the other side."

As he was describing this scene, he scribbled down this picture on a scrap piece of paper:

It's a pretty simple picture, right? At first glance, it may seem to have nothing to do with discipleship. But upon further reflection, you will see that it contains everything you need to know about discipleship. Curious? Let me explain...

I don't know how many of you are ocean swimmers or sailors, but any sailor or swimmer worth their weight knows that there are a few factors that you need to be aware of before embarking on an endeavor to cross the sea. In fact, if these factors are not taken into consideration, it could mean a disastrous journey before you even begin. And in the same way, there are a lot of factors that decide how far and how long we go in this discipleship journey that most people don't even think about before diving in.

So we are going to address the elements that can impact the depth and breadth of our Christlikeness as we swim or sail across the sea.

The Current. ≈

Anyone who has swum or sailed in the ocean knows about currents. I grew up in Vero Beach, which is a small beach town on the east coast of Florida and the house I grew up in was no more than one hundred yards from the Atlantic Ocean. There were many days when my friends and I would go down to the beach and swim and surf *all day*. Now we were all thoroughly educated by our parents about rip tides, currents, and the danger they presented. We could always tell how bad they were that day by how far down the beach we drifted while we swam or surfed. We would sometimes look up to realize that we were hundreds of yards down the beach from where we first started. The current is a subtle foe that slowly but surely moves you from where you want to go, even if that is simply maintaining your position, to somewhere you don't want to be. We have all heard the proverbial notion that if you are off by even one degree on a long journey, your destination may be hundreds of miles off your original mark. You must also recognize that if you do not account for the current, when making your calculations, you *will* be taken far away from your desired destination.

In your discipleship journey the current is your culture, your surroundings, and the things that pull at your time, your spiritual direction, and your overarching life and lifestyle. It is important to not just simply succumb to the current or pretend it is not there, but to use that awareness to not only combat the current but to also leverage it. You see, the pull of the waters is different in different geographical locations and in different seasons of life. A college student in Miami, Florida has a different current he/she is fighting against than a married woman with three kids in Gainesville, Florida. It doesn't mean one current is necessarily stronger or weaker than the other. It is, however, important for the college student to know what he/she is spiritually struggling against and for the married mom to know that the season she is in and the current she is battling is nothing like what she was going through as a college student.

Before you go on, turn to Appendix A, Section 1 and answer the questions about "The Current" in your life. It is important to do this now before you keep reading!

The Climate.

Sailing is one of the most weather-dependent sports. Any good sailor knows that *the* key element to a good day of sailing is the climate, and mainly the wind. There could be strong gusts of wind, a light breeze, or rainy squalls, each bringing about its own benefit or dilemma. But regardless of the type of wind, the fact remains that without the wind, there is a 100% guarantee that you are not going anywhere! You could have the sleekest sailboat and the best crew in the world, but without the wind you are stuck where you are. As much as sailing is in the hands of the sailor in regard to preparation and proper experience, it is just as dependent upon on the wind, climate, and conditions of the day.

The spiritual climate may not be as obvious as the wind when you are sailing in the middle of the sea, but it is equally as important. The wind of the Spirit, which way the Lord is moving, what He is up to, and where He is taking you, are questions that any disciple and disciple-maker is going to continually be asking himself/herself throughout the discipleship journey. "What is the Lord up to?" should be a question you ask yourself daily. Callings, ministry, and even everyday opportunities to step out in the name of Jesus are dependent upon whether or not your sails are up and the Holy Spirit is blowing wind into your sails.

My wife and I, for example, have an unequivocal call to missions that we both felt very strongly, even before we were married. That was one of the reasons I married Tracy! It is not too often that you meet a girl who is beautiful, smart, loves Jesus, AND doesn't mind living in a hut in the middle of nowhere for the rest of her life!! So when we got married, we prayed and prayed and asked God to send us... but we heard nothing. So we prayed some more... and heard nothing. We were honestly a little dejected because we *knew* that we were called, but the Lord simply wasn't calling us anywhere at the time. But looking back now almost ten years later, we both wholeheartedly agree that we would have been chewed up and spit out on the mission field if we'd gone in our early 20's. We just weren't ready. Now that doesn't mean that we don't still burn for the mission field; it just means that even though our sails were up, the wind wasn't blowing. We still feel the call and remain convinced that at some point we will be sent to the mission field. We are just waiting on the climate to change and the wind to pick up so we can be moving in step with the Spirit when we do!

Turn to Appendix A, Section 2 and answer the questions about "The Climate" in your life. It is important you do this now so it's fresh in your mind!

The Crew.

When you have the right crew, the simple but profound truth is that you simply get more done. You go farther, last longer, and are more productive when you work together, as opposed to working on your own. It is the principle of the slipstream and the draft. A slipstream is the region behind a moving object in which a wake of fluid (typically air or water) is moving at velocities comparable to the moving object, relative to the ambient fluid through which the object is moving. Drafting is the technique whereby two objects are caused to align in a close group, thereby reducing the overall effect of drag due to exploiting the lead object's slipstream. Drafting can significantly reduce the paceline's average energy expenditure required to maintain a certain speed and can also slightly reduce the energy expenditure of the lead object.

In layman's terms, when you work together, you get more done and exert less energy doing so.

Everybody wins.

But for whatever reason, a lot of us push back on this idea of finding the right crew and living life together. This is especially true in our spiritual walk because we have bought into the lie that our walk with Jesus is private, which is so far from Biblical, it's crazy! Your relationship with God may be personal but it is not, and was never meant to be, private. There are major detriments to your spiritual growth when you embrace the lone wolf mentality. Pursuing Jesus outside of a crew/community would be like swimming across the proverbial sea toward Christ at a ridiculously slow pace and saying to a ship that is *flying* by, "I don't need to sail with you guys; I am pretty content to swim by myself." Although swimming may feel comfortable because it is what you are used to doing and may make sense in the short run, it makes absolutely no sense in the long run. Sailing is going to get you there *exponentially* faster. Period.

Simply put, if you want to make substantial spiritual gains in this life, it is going to require finding and working with the right crew.

Think about it: have you ever made a promise to yourself that you would exercise more, go to the gym more regularly, or eat healthier? How long did that last? If you are like most of us, the answer is, "Not long". It is easy to put off internalized commitments because honestly, you really don't have any accountability. It is so much easier to justify being a slacker when it is all in your own mind instead of having to answer to someone else. Accountability makes us just that: accountable.

I can't tell you how many times I have committed, for example, to fasting in my mind and when I do it on my own I don't make it past noon on the first day! But when I verbalize my desire to fast to someone else, even the simple fact that I shared that out loud to someone else who is going to ask me about it makes it much more binding, and the probability of actually doing what I said is much greater.

But you have to have the right crew around you if you want to go deeper with Christ. "Show me your friends and I will show you your future" is something that rings true regardless of whether you are a teenager or an empty nester. You become like the people you are around.

So who exactly makes up this crew?

Your crew consists of the people with whom you are on this spiritual adventure. They are your microchurch family and the men or women you are discipling and living life with. They are the people who are sailing with you and the people who are lost, or swimming in the wrong direction, that you pick up along the way and point toward Jesus and say, "I have a better way! Follow me as I follow Christ. Join the crew!" and they do. You see, finding the right crew in one of the most important aspects of the discipleship journey!

> We will be addressing how to find and mobilize your crew at length in coming chapters.

The DiscipleSHIP.

Unless you are taking crazy pills, you would surely agree with me that sailing is a much more effective, efficient, and an overall better strategy for trying to cross the sea when compared to swimming. When a ship's crew works together as a unit they move faster, cover more ground, and expend less effort. Having ten people working together on a ship, each assigned to his/her responsibilities that contribute to the overall movement of the ship, will be hundreds of miles ahead of ten people trying to swim across the sea on their own within days. You would be a fool not to get on board, because the boat makes it possible for the collaborative whole to become far more valuable than its individual pieces. It is where we come together to develop and transform into something more than what we could be apart. You always hear in Christian circles to step out of the boat... but I am telling you to get into the boat!

So what exactly is the discipleSHIP? *It is how the church is forming around you.* It is the ship and the discipleship vehicle that you create with the crew that you have gathered. This could take the form of a discipleship group, a microchurch, a house church, or even the weekend gathering that you are a part of. It is the medium that you and your crew decide to create to help further advance the Gospel and make disciples together as a unit. This is where the rubber hits the road and you stop talking about doing something and *you actually do it.*

Now this explanation may leave more questions than answers, so in the last two chapters we are going to get extremely practical. We will be moving out of the vision and into the who, what, and how of discipleship and help you, step-by-step, start a discipleship revolution using the current, climate, crew, and the discipleSHIP that God is calling you to lead.

CHAPTER 3

ARE YOU READY?
The When

Paul tells the church of Corinth in 1st Corinthians 11:1 to "Follow me as I follow Christ." And sure, that is easy to say as arguably the most proficient church planter and disciple-maker of all time, right? But what about you? What is your reaction when you read that verse? Do you feel confident making that kind of bold proclamation to those around you?

If you are like the majority of most Christians I talk to, this verse is somewhat terrifying and it raises a ton of questions like, "There is so much of my life I would *not* want people following me in," or, "Maybe in a few years I might mature enough to say that, but not now, there's no way!" Whatever the reason, most Christians are hesitant to ask people to follow them as they follow Christ.

And this is one of the greatest lies Satan has successfully lodged into the hearts and minds of believers today.

With that in mind, let's go through a few of the most commonly perceived obstacles and excuses that hinder people from discipleship and why they simply are not true, shall we?

I Feel Too Unequipped To Disciple Someone! ─────

Let's look at the two greatest disciple-makers of all time: Jesus and Paul. Apparently neither of them had any problem releasing people to disciple who sometimes literally had just started following Jesus themselves... sometimes just minutes after their conversion!! Take the demoniac of Mark 5:1-20. Here is a guy who was a cutter, literally insane, and full of demons. He was also the guy who was delivered by Jesus and *immediately* released in Mark 5:19-20 to go share his story and make disciples. Now you might think, well, he was just sharing his story; that is different than discipleship. But I would argue that contextually, sharing his story *is* discipleship. This man is literally sharing all he knows about Jesus with everyone he meets! The action of disciple making often blends evangelism and what we would call post-conversion discipleship. It all falls under the banner of Matthew 28:18-20 when Jesus calls us to, "go make disciples of all nations, baptizing and teaching them to do everything I have commanded you." The first thing this guy did after he met Jesus was to go and make disciples! It is true, there was not a lot of equipping that took place before sending him out. He had his testimony, his encounter with Jesus, and with that he was off to make disciples.

The principle here is that you don't have to be a seminary grad to make disciples! Teach what you know, even if it is not that much! This is all that is required of you. As you teach, you will grow and learn more. As you learn more, you will begin to teach that, which will cause you to dive more deeply into prayer, the Scripture, the Spirit, etc. And before you know it, *discipleship will become one of the primary catalysts for your spiritual development.* They say the best way to learn is to teach. I am pretty sure Jesus had that in mind when He told us to make disciples... even when we don't feel equipped!

Paul also had rapid discipleship in mind wherever he went. There were times when he was only in a city for a few days or weeks, but that did not stop him from releasing his converts to evangelize and disciple! Scholars say that Paul would in some cases raise up elders in cities within a span of only a few months and set them over the church to lead.

Were they perfectly equipped? Hardly. Did they have issues? Just read the Bible. A good chunk of the New Testament writings was directed toward churches and people who were out of line! Paul was constantly trying to shepherd the flock, sometimes from afar with letters, and keep them moving in the right direction toward Christlikeness. But that brings up an underlying Biblical principle; it seemed like both Jesus and Paul were okay with people who were truly transformed by Jesus to start making disciples early in their walk with the Lord. They banked more on the Spirit's ability to keep people moving in the direction of holiness and godliness than on people's abilities to mess things up. Seeing every new believer as a potential and immediate disciple-maker is how church planting movements explode all over the world. When someone is raised in a spiritual community where evangelism and disciple making are an expectation *of all believers*, no matter how young in the faith, that community changes the world around them!

Note: Yes, there are cults and false teachers and people who have gone astray in major ways; I get that. But I also don't let fear dictate my discipleship, either. If you want to ensure proper orthodoxy and orthopraxy, discipleship should take place within the context of a church body with healthy spiritual theology and oversight.

My Life is So Messed Up; How Can I Possibly Ask Someone to Follow Me? ━━━━━━━━━━

Another thing Paul did not do was wait for perfection before releasing someone into his/her call to disciple. Paul was clearly okay with imperfect people making disciples. Paul did not say, "Follow me as I do it right," or "Follow me because I am amazing." He said, "Follow me *as I follow Christ*." This means there are things that Paul did well that people were expected to emulate. It also meant there were times when Paul blew it (see his relationship with Barnabas and John Mark)... but his shortcomings did not change his spiritual trajectory or his ability to follow Christ. I personally think it is *good* for your disciples to see that you are human, that you mess up, that you still make mistakes and have to ask for forgiveness.!

I remember playing ultimate Frisbee with some interns at our church and there was one guy in particular who was driving me crazy. He was running into everyone on the field, flagrantly fouling people with the Frisbee and wreaking havoc wherever he went. There was one time when he body-checked me while I had the Frisbee, but I was able to keep my cool. A few plays later, a teammate threw a high pass and I was fully extended in the air trying to make the catch, when this guy came right underneath me and cut my legs out from under me. I landed on the ground face first, twisted like a pretzel… and I honestly lost it. I got in his face and let off some verbal steam in a not so godly way because I was seething with anger and upset at his apparent inability to not knock people over. After I got myself together again I went over to him in front of all the other interns and people playing and apologized for my outburst.

The crazy thing is that a handful of the summer interns said that watching me lose it that night was the highlight of their internship! When I questioned them further, they replied, "It was so good to see that you are normal and that you do get upset like I do. I thought you never got upset about anything!" What a fail as a disciple-maker if the people I am overseeing don't think that real Christians ever get angry… that just isn't true! Does my anger get aroused less than it did before following Christ? Yes. Do I get less angry than I did even one year ago because of the work Christ is doing in my life? Absolutely, but that doesn't mean I don't ever get angry.

The point is this: people need to see the good, the bad, and the ugly. Every now and then the people you disciple need to see how you deal with life when it doesn't go well so they will get discipled in how to handle anger, for example, in a way that is going to honor Christ. Having people follow you as you follow Christ in regard to discipleship does not mean that you have it all together. It means that regardless of how good or bad your day is going or how put-together you feel, you are going to make a concerted effort to point your disciples to Jesus in all things and in all ways. It is better to be a disciple-maker who is still learning and growing than to not make disciples until you are perfect… because you and I both know that is never going to happen!

When To Pump the Brakes on Discipleship

Now this brings up a good point: is there ever a time when not making disciples is okay? Are there times or seasons in our lives when it is okay to not make that a priority? While my personal opinion is there are, I really think that there are only a few, which we will discuss below.

Life Emergencies & Unforeseen Struggles: My wife and I had an extremely difficult pregnancy and first few months with our first daughter. The long story short, our daughter has spina bifida so we did a fetal surgery out of state. This was followed by a ruptured membrane at 24 weeks which led to bed rest for 10 weeks in the hospital. After the birth, we spent another 11 days in the NICU. After that, my wife had three months of at-home quarantine because our little girl had a port put into her heart for medicine to combat a potential sickness she had.

The last thing I talked with my wife about was her lack of discipleship at that time. It simply wasn't a season for discipleship. Our primary focus was keeping our little girl alive! And there are going to be times in your life when the season you are in is simply not conducive to discipleship, so do not let condemnation creep into your heart if this is the case.

(Now we will be discussing in the next two chapters ways that discipleship can actually, as counter-intuitive as it seems, be the exact thing that helps to get you through hard seasons in ways that you might not think possible, such as when you are a new mom or going through hard times... so stay tuned!)

Major Sin Issues: Everybody sins and everybody has struggles. It's Biblical. We all fall short! But there are times when our personal life and pursuit of Jesus, our holiness and sanctification have to be our top priority. If there are deep sin issues in your life that you simply cannot shake and are bound in, then you need to focus on getting free and whole before bringing someone into your life for discipleship. When people try to make disciples while bound up in sin, it usually turns sour and ends up being very unfruitful. Do yourself and the people you want to disciple a favor and wait until you find freedom!

Summing It Up: How to Know When You Are Ready ——

If you are asking questions like, "But am I really ready to make disciples?" then you are probably closer to being ready than you think! I prefer when people have a small but healthy amount of caution and a strong desire to learn and grow in the process. The people I worry about the most are the ones who go into something like discipleship or marriage, for example, thinking that they won't have any issues and have it all together. (For anyone who is married, you know that they are in for a rude awakening!) Scriptures tell us to work out our salvation with fear and trembling, so I think it is safe to say we should do the same with discipleship!

With that being said, nothing helps boost your confidence like good confirmation from voices that you trust. I am a big proponent of being under spiritual authority, not in a weird or cultish way, but it is wise to have a few people in your life who are strong, mature disciples of Jesus that you give access to your life in regard to wisdom, prayer, and guidance. This could be a pastor, a microchurch leader, a family member, or a friend, but it needs to be someone you can trust to speak the truth in love to you. One of the best ways to know if you are ready or not is to ask! See if you and your spiritual authority agree that you are ready. If not, they can help you understand why and potentially help remove any barriers that may be keeping you from being ready for discipleship.

So if you have a medical crisis in your family, focus your attention there. If you are going through a divorce, let that settle and get healed before pulling people under your wings. It is okay to have major life issues and to focus your attention on them for a season, but don't let that put you into an eternal holding pattern. When the season has passed, and you and your spiritual authority both agree you're ready to get back in the game, go for it!

So what does this look like? How do you make disciples in *your* context? The next two chapters are going to give you an extremely practical and pragmatic approach to making disciples in *any* context and *any* season of life, so get ready to make this a reality!!

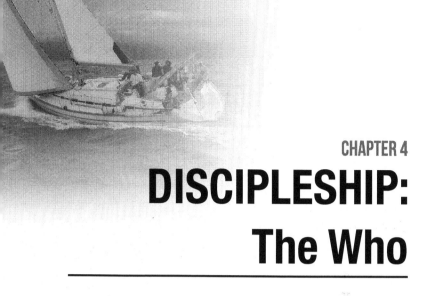

CHAPTER 4

DISCIPLESHIP:
The Who

The idea of making disciples, finding a crew, and creating a discipleSHIP in your life may seem like a very daunting one. It sounds like that would take a lot of effort and time. In fact, the number one reason why people say discipleship is not taking place in their lives is because they don't feel like they have the time for it. I did not address this concern in the last chapter when we talked about obstacles because I am going to spend the next two chapters addressing the lack of time issue specifically.

But what if I told you that you could be a part of a radical discipleship community and you wouldn't have to add one extra meeting to what you already do during your week? It's possible!! And I'm about to show you how, as we focus on finding your crew and creating your discipleSHIP.

The Fluidity of Finding the Crew and Creating the DiscipleSHIP

Trying to figure out which comes first, the crew or the discipleSHIP, is similar to asking the question, "Which came first, the chicken or the egg?" There is not a clear answer. In some cases, it is obvious that the people are the primary catalyst for discipleship and are chosen and prepared before the discipleSHIP is created. In other cases, the discipleSHIP is the driving force for recruitment and the primary way you find the right crew. It really just depends on how the Lord leads you. So in case you were wondering, we will be weaving in and out of crew and discipleSHIP talk throughout these next two chapters. Embrace the fluidity of the final steps!

Finding and Mobilizing Your Crew

Figuring out the current and climate of your discipleship journey are predominately an internal discovery that can be done on your own with some prayer and self-reflection. Finding your crew, however, is something that forces you to look outward and around you. If you are just starting out, it may seem like an overwhelming task to go find these people, befriend them, and convince them to join you in your journey toward Jesus.

But the beauty is that the majority of the time, your crew is already a part of your life... *they just need to be mobilized.*

Again, discipleship is not about adding to your plate; *it is about assimilating people and discipleship opportunities into what you are already doing.* There is a huge difference!! With a bit of intentionality, you can breathe life into seemingly mundane and routine parts of your day by bringing people along with you and incorporating discipleship.

Jesus was extremely creative and a master of taking His surroundings and conversations, whatever they might have been, and turning them into a discipleship lesson where drew people into the Kingdom reality and way of life. Whether He was in a rural town talking about seeds, crops, or baking materials (Matthew 13:1-35) or in the city using the money in His hands (Mark 12:17), He always found a way to relate everyday life to God and His Kingdom. This is a critical art of discipleship that has been lost in a very unimaginative and predictable 21st century. We need to learn how to creatively breathe Kingdom life into everyday activities!! All it takes is some practice and imaginative effort. You could easily turn a typical study time with your fellow college classmates into a discipleship moment through intentional conversation. You could turn the time you play with your newborn into a chance for other moms to connect with you and with Jesus. You could transform lunch at work into an inductive Bible study with your coworkers. With a little bit of ingenuity, discipleship can be happening anywhere you want it to!

Now it is one thing to have a good imagination and the ability to think of abstract discipleship concepts that relate to everyday life... but that doesn't mean anything if you have no one to share it with!! So one of the key questions when it comes to discipleship is *who* are you going to do this with? The answer to this question is easier than you may initially think. It comes from the Greek word "oikos". This word oikos means "house" or "household". In the first century, it meant a person's family, slaves, and, through their network of relationships, friends, neighbors and even business associates. The early church was predominately established through these social and relational pathways, and the discipleship network that you are going to be a part of will primarily come through these types of relationships, as well.

Stop reading for a second a flip to Appendix A, Section 3 under "The Crew" and answer questions 10 & 11 about the people you are closest to during this season of your life. This will help you start to define your oikos!

Note: the ten names you wrote down are just a primer. These could or could not be the best people for you to start a discipleSHIP with. Most likely one or two of these people will be part of the crew, but don't limit yourself to just these people. Think of anyone else whom God has put in your path who may be open to jumping in to what you may be starting. It might even be that your discipleSHIP (whether that is working out, leading a dad's breakfast before work, praying in the morning, having a weekly game of softball followed by a time of discipleship) begins to become the recruiting force for your discipleship journey.

Discipleship Formats and Making the Ask ————

If you are a crew-first type of person and what you do is not as important as whom you do it with, then we need to get into the details of how to make "the ask", an often overlooked part of discipleship. It feels awkward and pretentious for most people to stroll up to someone and ask, "Do you want me to disciple you?" There must be a better way, right? And there is. But first, you as the disciple-maker need to know what you yourself are asking! What type of discipleship are you offering and expecting? There are a variety of forms of discipleship that one can be a part of. Which is best for you in this season, however, is another critical question. Here is a short list of the types of discipleship we see taking place in the New Testament. Each one can be emulated with great success today.

Spiritual Fathers/Mothers: This is what most people think of when they hear discipleship: someone with way more experience, grey hair, and wisdom than the person being discipled. Think of pouring out into the younger generation. Think of Paul and Timothy. Moses and Aaron. Yoda and Luke Skywalker. In this scenario, the disciple-maker is clearly years ahead of the protégé in regard to spiritual maturity, and the authority of the teacher is undisputed.

When This Works: If you are, in fact, years ahead of someone in their walk with the Lord. It can work with a younger disciple-maker and older disciples, but these circumstances are rare. It also works with a relatively mature disciple who is discipling a brand new Christian.

When This Doesn't Work: This is a hard model to follow if you are discipling peers and there is not a clear delineation of authority between or among those participating. A Bible study for college students led by another college student is an example of when this model wouldn't really work.

Making the Ask: In this scenario, there is no awkwardness about asking someone if they would like to be discipled because it is clear to both the disciple and disciple-maker who would be the leader and who would be the disciple. It is as simple as saying, "I was praying through discipleship and the Lord brought you to mind. Would you be interested in doing some discipleship with me?"

Relational Discipleship: Relational discipleship works on the premise that there is more equality in the relationship of the two or more parties involved. This is more peer-based discipleship, with all parties on close-to-equal footing spiritually. We see this type of discipleship in the New Testament church among the apostles. After Jesus ascended, the apostles worked together and collaborated to ensure that the mission of Jesus was carried out by the early church. Paul even came before his peers in Jerusalem and confirmed that the Gospel he was preaching to the Gentiles was in line with what the twelve apostles deemed correct in Acts 21.

In relational discipleship, there may be one person who is more spiritually mature, but it is usually not by much. It follows more along the lines of focusing on a strong accountability and an iron-sharpens-iron type of approach, but with the mutual agreement and interest of going deeper in the Lord through this forged relationship.

When This Works: This is a great format for people in the same season of life: college students, young moms/dads, professionals, empty nesters, etc. The relational approach may have a designated leader, but that does not have to be the case. Usually it involves a medium that can be mutually edifying and doesn't require a strong leader, such as reading through a book of the Bible or a book having to do with discipleship in the season of life the members are in.

When This Doesn't Work: This model is difficult when there is a clear leader who carries weight in their personal walk with the Lord and has a spiritual maturity that transcends the others in the group. If positioned as a relational discipleship group, it will naturally become a spiritual father/mothering group, which can cause strife and/or if this was not the original vision.

Making the Ask: As the name suggests, the premise of this type of approach is relational. The ask should be something along the lines of, "Hey I was thinking about getting a few people together to grow and encourage one another in our walks with Jesus. Would you be interested in something like that?" It may also be followed by a conversation of what you all think would be a good resource to use together to encourage the equal footing aspect of this group.

Workplace Discipleship: Paul was the master at this. He was able to weave his work and his ministry into one fluid lifestyle and leveraged his time "in the workplace" to share the Gospel and encourage other believers, like

Priscilla and Aquila, who were also tentmakers. We all want to be like Paul and be salt and light in our workplace, but how does this flesh itself out? This is one way to do it! Workplace discipleship usually revolves around an open group setting where both believers and unbelievers can sit down, usually before or after work, or at lunchtime, to share about their faith and/or to read through a book or book of the Bible. As the leader of this crew, you have major flexibility of how evangelistic you want this to be. But the crew and the time you meet is almost chosen for you since it will be the people you work with during the times that you all have a break.

When This Works: This can be an awesome way to meet other Christians and reach out to those who are far from God, especially if you work in a large company, hospital, school, etc. It is a great way to sharpen and encourage one another in the workplace and acts as an easy way to use invitational evangelism to its fullest potential since it is literally as easy as walking to the lunch or break room. There is also a definitive start and end time, so it is an easy yoke for you as a leader.

When This Doesn't Work: This can be difficult in work environments with limited time to meet together (commuter jobs, short lunch breaks, etc.) It can also be challenging in a small office where the CEO or manager is anti-religion or disapproves of such meetings.

Making the Ask: This is a really simple ask for the other Christians in your office: "Hey, I am thinking about starting up a weekly Bible study at lunch on Tuesdays. It could be a really cool way for us to encourage one another and stay spiritually sharp throughout the week. Would you like to jump in?!"

For those far from God in the office, you might switch up your approach and say something along the lines of, "Hey, I am going to be starting a book club on Tuesdays at the office. Some weeks we are going to be diving into spiritual things, other weeks we are just going to be hanging out and getting to know other people in the office. Would you be interested in something like that?"

Ministry Based Discipleship: I love how radically Paul gave himself to discipleship and the advancement of the Gospel. Everywhere he went, disciples were being made. If he came to a city without a church, you better believe by the time he left, there was one! But this meant the raising up of elders and leaders to care for the flock and to further propagate the Gospel once he was gone. This type of ministry-based discipleship usually happens within the church context or in a discipleSHIP context that has a specific ministry focus. This could be with kid's church, a youth group, in a microchurch setting, or even a house church. Think about what ministry you are involved in and think through if there are opportunities for you to disciple someone in that context.

This also works outside the church where people are doing ministry at a juvenile detention center, in the jails and prisons, on the streets to the homeless or women vulnerable to prostitution. Wherever this type of discipleship might be happening, it is centered on the ministry at hand and raising someone up in that context to be a good, strong, healthy disciple-maker.

When This Works: This obviously only works when there is a ministry that can be the primary focus of the discipleship taking place. There also needs to be someone well versed in the ministry who can impart the knowledge and tools necessary for the disciple to succeed. Pretty straight forward here!

When This Doesn't Work: This does not work if there is no ministry to use as the foundation for this discipleship relationship.

Making the Ask: The ask is often done for you since new people wanting to lead in your ministry usually have some sort of process to go through before they can become leaders in your ministry.

Stop and take a second to think through what kind of discipleship would work best for you in this season of life. Then go to question 12 in "The Crew" section of Appendix A and check off all that might apply.

The Two Sides of Discipleship: Organized and Organic

As much as I want to ensure that discipleship works in your season of life and the context you are currently in, I also want to ensure that well-rounded discipleship is taking place. In order for this to happen, I believe that discipleship needs to be both organized and organic. There are key elements that happen better in organic settings and others that flourish when the setting is organized and well planned. Let me break that down:

Organic: The organic side of discipleship has to do with relationships. Organic discipleship happens in the moments when you "catch" someone being a disciple simply because you are living life with them. How much you tip a waitress, how you respond when your two year old throws a temper tantrum, when you get utterly crushed in a sporting event, when you have dinner at someone's home and watch them interact with their family, or see them witnessing to someone as you work out... these are the moments when organic discipleship takes place. It is someone watching a disciple live out his/her faith in everyday life. Much like a child imitates his/her parent in regard to the words they say and the way they act, organic discipleship is likened to that type of intimate imitation, simply by being around someone long enough to see the fruit in their life.

Organized: The organized side of discipleship has to do with intentional, thought-out times of teaching and instruction. Usually this happens at a scheduled, weekly meeting between a disciple and a disciple-maker when prayer, Bible study, and teaching take place. Other more organized gatherings, such as a microchurch, fall into the category of organized discipleship, as well.

Good discipleship and good discipleSHIPs are going to have both of these components. If a moms' group is just a hang-out time with each other at the mall playground while their kids play (an organic touch) but never gets to spiritual disciplines or intentional conversations about discipleship (organized component), then this is lacking. If someone rallies a bunch of guys together to go biking every Saturday morning (organic time together), but the time ends there (lacking organized time together), we are missing a critical piece of the equation. Conversely, if a group meets at the church in the mornings and has amazing times of prayer and memorizes Scripture together (organized) but never sees each other outside of the context of organized discipleship (no organic touches), this is also lacking in regard to holistic discipleship. The key is knowing what your tendency is and leaning into that, while not neglecting the other side of discipleship!

What are you? More organized or organic? Flip to question 13 in Appendix A to check off which applies before you move on!

CHAPTER 5

DiscipleSHIP:
The How

The church is not the brick and mortar building we meet in on Sundays. It is not the programs that take place throughout the week. These are merely by-products of the church. So what is the church?

You are the church.

When you find a group of Jesus-followers who are devoted to worship, mission, and community, you find the church. This brings us to a critical question in regard to discipleship and your discipleSHIP: *how is the church forming around you?*

Forming the discipleSHIP: How the Church is Organically Forming Around You ─────────────

This is where you are going to personally start tying things together. Go ahead and flip over to Appendix A and start readdressing and processing through your current, climate, and crew questions, because these are going to be great indicators and starting points for the formation of your discipleSHIP from an organic discipleship perspective.

In order to help you do this, let's imagine a new mom as an example of someone who is going through this book and is trying to form her discipleSHIP. This might be the way she responds to the previous questions concerning her current, climate, and crew. As we use her as an example, follow along with your own notes and come to your own discipleSHIP conclusions:

Current:

- *How can your season of life and what is drawing you to God be shared with others?*

    * Ex: One way a young mom could take advantage of her season would be to connect with other young moms around the topic of motherhood and how they are seeing God move in unique ways that moms experience.

- *How can you overcome or even form a group when you are facing roadblocks that seem to be keeping you from God?*

  * Ex: Childcare is a major obstacle, not having enough time to seek the Lord, and feeling unequipped are all obstacles that could keep her from discipling.

  * With that in mind, maybe this mom could host a playgroup at her house so all the moms could discuss tactics and ways to seek the Lord when trying to care for a newborn. They could have accountability about this and maybe read something beforehand to discuss as the kids are playing.

SIDENOTE: It is important to understand that the different seasons of life are going to be just that: different. Comparing your life as a parent to when you were involved in a college ministry is comparing apples to oranges. Of course your time with the Lord is going to look different. Yes, you have less time as a parent than a college student. And discipleship will look different as an empty nester than it did when you had kids. Accepting and embracing that fact will very much help your discipleship journey in this season of your life. The Lord will work with what you have, so be open to discipleship, even if it doesn't look like it has in the past!

Climate:

This is a key part of your discipleSHIP. You want to form the church around you in the areas that you are passionate about, have a calling, are excited about, or have a passion to change. It is about paving the sidewalk where you are already walking.

So what is that for you?

Do you love working out? Do you love reading books? Do you love sports, painting, poetry, or coffee? Do you enjoy contemplative prayer and journaling? Whatever you love, is there a way to bring people along with you in that passion and incorporate discipleship into that? Here are some examples:

- Working out: If you love working out, you could launch an early morning or late night workout with a handful of people. Each person comes ready to share what God has been doing in his or her life that week and in between sets, the group can review the Scripture they are memorizing together. As you are drinking a protein shake or eating afterwards, you could review a book of the Bible you are reading together.

- Reading books: If you are a book lover, start a book club with a spiritually geared book, inviting both non-believers and believers over for dinner once a week.

- Sports: If you are an avid sports player, you could have a consistent time of the week when you play a sport together on a city league and reach out to those playing with you who are not believers. After the sport, you could spend some more focused discipleship time with a core team as you grab a bite to eat.

A fun fact is that all of these discipleship illustrations are real life examples! Each consists of a different approach and discipleSHIP, but each is moving toward the goal of making disciples who make disciples. The important thing is to tie discipleship into something that you are already doing and have a passion for, whether that has spiritual implications or not. It is your job to creatively bring discipleship elements into that passion of yours, so that it truly becomes a discipleSHIP.

If you are reading this section and are thinking, "I don't have time for this type of stuff", ask yourself why you feel that way and then ask if there is a way to form a discipleSHIP around the roadblock to discipleship. For example, I have some friends that were microchurch leaders but then they adopted two boys, and this took up every ounce of their extra time. They had to pull back from microchurch leadership and hand the reigns off to someone else. This felt like a major setback for them discipleship-wise, until they started to form a discipleSHIP around their journey with their adopted sons! Now they help facilitate a support group centered around accountability and encouragement for other parents who have also adopted children.

You have to remember that sometimes the things which look like the greatest setbacks are the very things God is calling you to use as the foundation of your discipleSHIP!

By the way, if you are more of an in-the-box type of person, then embrace that! It is totally okay to do discipleship in a more traditional set up. Don't feel like you have to make it flashy or unique for the sake of being trendy. If you want to meet with guys early in the morning for prayer together at the church and then do discipleship there, which is what I do, go for it. Nothing fancy or new about that, but hey, it works for my family's schedule. That way when I do the majority of my discipleship before they wake up. Again, it all depends on what works for you.

Forming the discipleSHIP: How Are You Organizing the Church Around You?

Now that we have hammered out a lot of ways to organically connect with people who are potentially in similar seasons, have similar interests, spiritual pursuits, etc, it's time to put some organized discipleship teeth to your discipleSHIP. This ensures that there is also an element of spiritual progression when you meet with the people you are wanting to disciple and not just making social connections that don't lead you any closer to Christ. Don't get me wrong; there is nothing bad about social connections, but that is not the same thing as discipleship. Flag football with friends is a social hangout if there is no organized discipleship. Breakfast with other businessmen or businesswomen is simply a social endeavor if there is no organized discipleship driving that connection. We are not looking for social hangouts; we are looking for disciples who are going to make more disciples, and the intentional injection of organized discipleship into organic gatherings is what makes that happen.

Organizing Around The Great Commandment & The Great Commission

Let's go back to the beginning shall we? Each discipleSHIP should be in line with God's will for your life, thereby fulfilling these two Biblical calls and hitting the three categories of balanced, comprehensive discipleship: worship, mission, and community. How do you ensure that all three of these components are covered in a discipleship and discipleSHIP context? Well, I am glad you asked! Below are ways that you can assimilate each of these key components of organized discipleship into your discipleSHIP:

*Core **Worship** Components of a DiscipleSHIP*

- **Prayer** is foundational when it comes to good discipleship. You really get to know someone's heart when you hear him or her pray. You also learn how to pray by hearing others pray. Prayer is caught more than it is taught, so make sure this is a part of your discipleSHIP!

- **The Word/Study material** is another key aspect of organized discipleship. Getting someone grounded in the Bible or Biblical truth is what is going to change him or her, so choose a study that is relevant to your Crew. Ask yourself: what are the spiritual needs of my Crew? What would sharpen them and help them grow to become stronger disciples in their context? Do you and the Crew need to go through the book of James? Do they need to read a book on seeking the Lord? Should you go through a study on evangelism? Find out the needs and address them!

- **Scripture memorization** is one of the massively potent foundations of strong discipleship. All over the Word, we see the fruit of this endeavor (Hebrews 4:12, Psalm 119:9, Psalm 119:11, Joshua 1:8-9, to name a few) and the power of having the Word written on your heart. Please don't miss this! Incorporate it into whatever you are doing!!

> Flip on over to Appendix A, question 15, and integrate some worship ideas into your discipleSHIP model.

*Core **Mission** Components of a DiscipleSHIP*

- **Evangelism** is one of those abilities of strong disciples that will sometimes get swept under the rug if you yourself are not an evangelist. But make sure that you are doing the people you are discipling a favor and implement evangelism in your discipleSHIP model. Start praying for the lost together, taking turns sharing the Gospel, however that plays itself out! Just make sure you are doing it.

- **Justice** is another great element that usually comes into play if the disciple-maker has a passion about a specific issue. Your discipleship may be taking place on your way to the prisons to share there, or on the streets with the homeless or women vulnerable to prostitution.

- **Service and generosity** are always good for the soul. Making sure people are actively serving their community and giving generously will break up hard hearts. Actively pursuing this with your disciples is always a good idea.

Turn to Appendix A, question 16, and integrate some missional ideas into your discipleSHIP model.

*Core **Community** Components of a DiscipleSHIP*

- **Accountability** is a great way to form strong intimate connections with the people you are discipling. Getting to know their struggles, lifting them up, bearing each other's burdens, prayerfully pushing back darkness and celebrating spiritual victory will draw you together, without question.

- **Multiple Touches.** Since community itself is a given, multiple touches a week with your disciples ensure that you are actually allowing enough time for both organized and organic discipleship to take place. Sure, you may have your weekly organized time together, but the more that your disciples can "catch" you being a disciple, the better. The more times that they can see you outside of an official meeting, the better. Let people in so that they can see you, your family, and your life as it really is. These are some of the most powerful discipleship moments; watching a passionate follower of Jesus do day-to-day things! It might not seem like a big deal to you, but trust me, I can say from experience that this is a huge deal for someone you are discipling!

Go to Appendix A, question 17, and integrate these community ideas into your discipleSHIP model.

Don't Just Build a Ship. Build An Armada!!

One key element that is often overlooked in a healthy discipleship model is the idea of outreach and multiplication within a discipleship context. Discipleship is not just about pulling your Christian friends together so you can hang out another time during the week (although this absolutely is a by-product)! Discipleship is about making disciples, but it's not only about making disciples. It is about making disciple-makers... and there is a HUGE difference!!

So if you are a disciple-maker and you want your disciples to actually be real-deal disciples, according to the Great Commission, they need to be making disciples themselves, not just be on the receiving end of your discipleship! Part of true discipleship is the propagation of discipleship. Second Timothy 2:2 says, "What you have heard me say in the presence of many witnesses, entrust to reliable men who will also be qualified to teach others." You want to make sure there is a strong, clear call to the people you are discipling so that after your time of discipleship is over, *there is an expectation that they are going to go and do the same!!*

Here are some very practical ways to ensure that this happens:

- **Keep a running VIP list.** A VIP list is a list of the "Very Important People" in your life who do not yet know Jesus that you are praying would come to know and follow Him. Have each person in your discipleship group pray for these people in his/her life every time you meet. Keep evangelism in front of them at all times. Best-case scenario: they can start a discipleSHIP with the people that come to the Lord through their evangelism and outreach!

- **Ask Early and Often: "Who Are *You* Going to Disciple?"** It is amazing how much a simple question like this can be a game changer. The majority of the time, when you ask someone you are discipling who they are going to disciple, you get a blank stare and an open mouth. Most people have never thought about who they would disciple. By even asking this question, you are starting to help your disciples have a 2nd Timothy 2:2 mentality and it gets them actively looking for those to disciple. Walk them through the process of finding disciples and pray with them for this to take place!

- **Have a Commissioning Ceremony.** Let your disciples know that once your discipleship time with them is complete, the expectation is that they are going to go and make disciples of their own! Let this be a guiding vision your entire time together. One way to make this special is to anoint them and pray for them as a commissioning to go make disciples of their own. This adds an element of importance, significance, and spiritual authority to what you are asking them to do.

Now that you have walked through why this matters, what Jesus is calling you to, when you are ready for discipleship, who you are going to be discipling, and how you are going to do it, let's bring this all together into a personalized discipleship and discipleSHIP plan! Refresh yourself with a look at your answers in Appendix A, read through a few different discipleSHIP models in Appendix B, and then finally turn over to Appendix C to formulate your discipleSHIP!

Appendix A: Putting It All Together

In order to maximize this booklet and help you begin or hone in on your discipleship journey, you will need to think through the following questions and answer honestly! This is about where you are, not where you IDEALLY want to be. Don't try to impress anyone with your answers or you will create a false reality of your situation that is not helpful to you in regard to disciple making and launching your discipleSHIP with your newfound crew!

SECTION 1: THE CURRENT

Personal

1. What season of life are you in? (Ex: college focused, motherhood, career oriented, empty nesters... you can put as many as you feel are applicable)

    _____

2. How is this season drawing you closer to God? (If it is not, say that too!)

    _____

    _____

    _____

3. How is this season pushing you away from God?

    _____

    _____

    _____

Disciple Making

4. What do you feel are the biggest roadblocks or
   hindrances that are keeping you from making
   disciples? (Not enough time, can't find a babysitter,
   don't feel equipped, etc.)

- _____

- _____

- _____

- _____

- _____

SECTION 2: THE CLIMATE

5. Do you feel like you have a calling? Who are you called to/what do you feel like you are called to do?

    It is okay if you don't have a clear calling on your life just yet. The next few questions will hopefully help hone that in a bit if you don't already!

    _____

    _____

    _____

6. List out a few things that you are passionate about.

    This could be a hobby (sports, knitting), a spiritual discipline (the Word, prayer), a people group (other fathers, the poor, your kids), a cause (racial reconciliation, foster parenting, cancer survivors)

    - _____

    - _____

    - _____

    - _____

7. What makes you angry, cry, or frustrated when you think about the situation?

   This doesn't necessarily have to be spiritual, although it definitely can be!

   • _____

   • _____

   • _____

8. What do you get excited thinking about? What do you daydream about doing?

   This doesn't necessarily have to be spiritual, although it definitely can be!

   • _____

   • _____

   • _____

9. What do you feel like the Lord is saying to you right now in this season? Does anything feel like it is a "word from the Lord" or a confirmation to move forward with something at this time?

- _____

- _____

- _____

Talk it Out!

Begin to activate your vision by talking this out with someone else. Vision does not get birthed if you keep it in the womb. You need to speak it out, share it, and put yourself out there by speaking it out to others. Vision is only vision if it is shared. *Activate* your vision by sharing it with someone else.

Even if you are not sure what it is yet, find someone to dream with. You will be amazed at how much traction comes with the sharing of vision via a good brainstorming session with someone who wants to see you succeed and become who God wants you to be! So go and find that friend and see if they have any input with any of these questions that you may have missed!

SECTION 3: THE CREW

10. List the top 10 people that you have the closest relationship with in your life right now who live in the same town that you do. They could be friends, family (outside of your nuclear family), coworkers, neighbors, classmates, church friends, etc. They could be followers of Jesus or not! Do not limit this just to Christians.

1. _____

2. _____

3. _____

4. _____

5. _____

6. _____

7. _____

8. _____

9. _____

10. _____

11. If you did not already include them in your top ten, write down 3-10 people you have the closest relationship with who are not yet following Jesus. This could be friends, neighbors, classmates, people you have gotten to know at stores or restaurants you frequent often, etc.

1. _____

2. _____

3. _____

4. _____

5. _____

6. _____

7. _____

8. _____

9. _____

10. _____

12. Check which type(s) of discipleship model are you seeking to pursue or you think would work best for your discipleSHIP model.

☐ Spiritual Father/Mother

☐ Relational Discipleship

☐ Workplace Discipleship

☐ Ministry Based Discipleship

☐ Other: _____

13. Are you more prone to leading organic or organized discipleship? (It's just good to know so that you are aware if you are leaning too heavily toward your natural tendency.) Check one:

☐ I am more comfortable with organic, get to know you type of environments.

☐ I thrive when there is structure and an organized agenda with people.

SECTION 4: DiscipleSHIP

14. How is the church organically forming around you based on the current and climate of your life in this season? What passions, callings, or hobbies would you enjoy and be energized by rallying people around? This could be as large scale as doing something to combat sex slavery to as simple as meeting up with friends your age for coffee or to play sports. List the top five things you would enjoy doing with others:

1. _____

2. _____

3. _____

4. _____

5. _____

15. Worship Focus of Your DiscipleSHIP: In what ways are you going to be incorporating worship? Check all that apply:

☐ Prayer together

☐ Reading the Word

- What book of the Bible are you considering?

  _____

☐ Reading a book

- What book are you considering? What would fit with your Crew or season of life?

  ▪_____

- Some suggestions:

  * *The Real Deal* by Mike Patz is an amazing resource for new believers (you can find it on www.greenhousechurch.org)

  * *The Green Book or Fluent: A Practical Guide for Disciples Who Make Disciples* by Matt Ulrich, are great for general discipleship (you can find these on Amazon.com)

☐ Memorizing Scripture

16. Mission Focus of Your DiscipleSHIP: how are you encouraging your disciples to be or stay on mission? Check all that apply:

☐ Evangelism will be a regular part of what we do together.

☐ We will be praying together for those far from God to come to know Him.

☐ We will be actively involved in justice issues.

- What types of justice issues? _____
  _____

☐ We will be serving our community together.

- What are some service ideas you have? _____
  _____

☐ We will be giving toward a specific cause or concern together

- What types of causes? _____
  _____

17. Community Focus of Your DiscipleSHIP

☐ Accountability will be a part of our discipleSHIP.

☐ I am going to try to have multiple touches a week with my disciples.

- Are there any times you want to lock in as times you will spend with your disciples on a weekly basis? (Ex: Dinner at your house every Monday, praying together every Thursday morning, running together Saturday mornings, etc.)

- _____
  _____
  _____

Appendix B: Current and Creative Models

Think of these discipleSHIP models like training wheels. Much like children have training wheels on their bikes until they can learn to ride without them, these templates can give you that creative spark you need to begin a discipleSHIP model. If it will help, borrow and implement some ideas below that are going to help you get your discipleSHIP in the water. Or just utilize this as a way to get the creative juices flowing! Here are a variety of discipleSHIP models that have been successfully put into practice and are still going on here in Florida and have served as catalysts for winning people to the Lord and making disciples:

1. Basketball League: Jared, a working father of three, loved playing basketball and played in his spare time. He was looking for a way to have an outlet to invite unbelievers into the life of a believer, so he created a basketball league. The microchurch leaders of our church were the captains and formed teams with other microchurch members along with their unbelieving friends and others who just wanted to play basketball. It is in its third season and has seen many guys get connected into microchurches and discipled as a result.

2. Juvenile Detention Center Outreach: Murray, a retired professor from the University of Florida, has a heart for young men who have been incarcerated. For decades Murray has gone every Monday night and preached to, prayed for, and ministered to the boys in the juvie center. Murray was going there anyway, but he decided to start asking if other men wanted to go and minister with him. He currently has anywhere from 2-12 guys who go with him on Mondays, and they have been discipled in outreach, preaching the Gospel, and ministering to this unique population of our city.

3. Outreach to Women Vulnerable to Prostitution: Alison, a mother of five, could not shake the desire to do something to help women involved in the sex industry, but with five kids, she couldn't' up and leave her home here in Gainesville. So she decided to do something locally, forming a team of men and women around her that do regular outreaches to women on the streets, in strip clubs and other venues where sex trafficking runs rampant.

4. Seasonal Microchurch. Matt and Tracy, a couple in their early thirties, began leading a microchurch when they were newly married and in their mid twenties, reaching predominately college students and young professionals. As their family has increased from just the two of them to now the four of them (two children later), their microchurch has also shifted to a young families group, as they continue to minister to people who share the same season of life as they do.

5. Breakfast and the Bible. Joel is a father of two and the CEO of a mid-sized company who, during busy seasons, is out of town upwards of 5 days a week. Joel, however, meets with a core group of guys for discipleship once a week early in the morning for breakfast, discipleship, and accountability. If he is away on business, one of the other guys he has helped to raise up leads in his absence.

6. Home School Co-Op. Katie is a mom of three and is home schooling her children. Instead of home schooling on her own, she created a home school co-op with other families where Bible study is not only a part of the children's curriculum, but also a part of the parents' time together as well! It has become a family hub of not only scholastic learning but discipleship, as well!

7. Artistic Gathering with Spiritual Roots. Once a month, Jymi invites other artists (some believers, some not) to paint a spiritual theme together. Each woman is provided with her own canvas and paints and they paint together as they meditate on one of the fruits of the Spirit or some other spiritual focal point, which is their muse for painting.

8. Entrepreneurial Discipleship. Czar, a father of three, moved down to South Florida to accept a full time job and realized there was a vacuum of discipleship in his area. So he started a microchurch and invited some friends. That microchurch multiplied and then multiplied again. Soon the microchurches were gathering to meet as a house church. This grew and the microchurches continued to multiply, so they launched a weekend service and planted a macrochurch to come alongside their microchurches!

Appendix C:
Discipleship Mad Libs

Remember when you were little (or maybe still) and you would do mad libs by writing down all these random nouns, verbs, and adjectives and then insert them into a story for some really weird and sometimes awkward conclusions? Well, think of this as your discipleship mad libs. You are going to be taking everything you wrote in Appendix A and putting it into a concise and hopefully helpful (instead of awkward) conclusion in regard to forming your Crew and your DiscipleSHIP, so get ready to flip back and forth between Appendixes A & C and bring your discipleSHIP together!!

As you start writing these down, your answers might change a bit based on how your discipleSHIP is forming. Once you see it all in one place, it might take a different shape or be with different people than you thought, and that is okay! The goal is for you to feel confident in moving forward with discipleship, so use this as a way to help you figure that out!

Look at Appendix A, questions 1-9 and question 14. Synthesize your thoughts and answer the following question:

My discipleSHIP is going to be formed around _____

_____

_____

_____

Look at your answer for question 12:

The type of discipleship that best fits my discipleSHIP is: _____

Look at your answers for questions 10 & 11:

The 2-5 people that would be the best fit for this discipleSHIP are:

1. _____

2. _____

3. _____

4. _____

5. _____

Look at your answer for question 14:

Some ways I can organically interact with my disciples are:

1. _____

2. _____

3. _____

4. _____

5. _____

Look at your answer for question 15-17:

What book of the Bible, book, or curriculum are you planning on studying with your disciples?

_____

What other ways will you be incorporating the worship element into your discipleSHIP?

_____

_____

_____

What about mission?

_____

_____

_____

And community?

_____

_____

_____

Where and when would be a good time during your week to have an organized meet with your disciples? (Ex. Tuesdays at 7am at Starbucks)

_____

51610101R00057

Made in the USA
Lexington, KY
29 April 2016